Teacher

Margaret Hudson

Contents

Heinemann

Where in the world?

Everyone needs to learn to read, write and count. All over the world there are different people who teach us these things.

We are going to visit four of these people. The children they teach are all in their first four years at school.

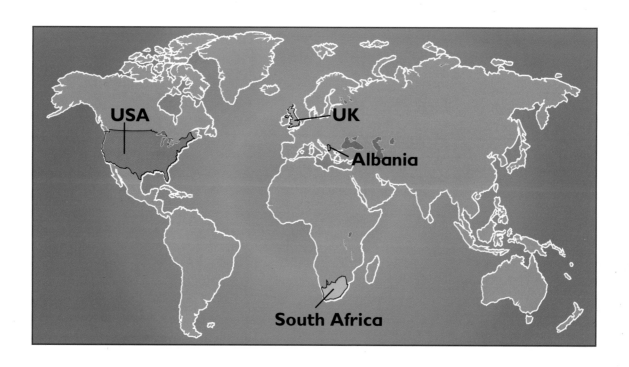

Charlotte teaches 6 and 7 year olds in **first grade** in a school in Boston, in the United States of America (USA).

Entela teaches in a **primary** school in Shkodra, Albania. Her **students** are 8 and 9 years old.

Ian teaches in a primary school in Doncaster, in the United Kingdom (UK). His students are 8 and 9 years old.

Sylvia teaches 5, 6 and 7 year olds in a primary school in Mitchells Plain, South Africa.

Teaching you

Schools are different in different countries. They are even different in the same country.

Charlotte's school was built in 1907. A lot of work was done on the school in 1991. There is an **adventure playground** for the children to play on.

Entela's school is in an old building. There is not enough money to make the school look smart. But there is plenty of room for the children to play.

More children go to Ian's school now
than when it was built, in 1968. Ian
teaches in a **mobile classroom** on
the playground.

Sylvia's school is the newest of all the
schools. It was built in the 1970s, at the
same time as most of the houses around
it. So it has lots of space for playing and
sport.

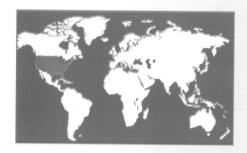

USA

Charlotte Clements-Hailey has to be at school to start work at 8.30 in the morning. She lives 45 minutes' drive away from the school. Her daughter, Talya, goes to the **local** school.

The school day lasts from 8.30 am until 2.30 pm. The children have their lunch early, at about 11.30 am.

Here Charlotte is talking to all the
children while they sit on the carpet.
The **class** often start the day like this.

The **students** talk about the things they
have learned and the work they will do
during the day. Charlotte teaches them to
read and write. She also teaches them
maths and science. They learn about
other countries too.

The students learn other things too. They do **P.E.** They learn music. Here Charlotte is teaching Amanual and Kathleen to play the recorder. They are learning how to play the tune 'Mary had a Little Lamb'.

While Charlotte teaches the recorder, the rest of the **class** work at their desks. Today they are using **workbooks**. They are doing work on sounds and spelling.

The family eat their main meal together
in the evening. Charlotte's mother,
Mrs Clements, lives with Charlotte
and Talya.

Here Charlotte and Talya are eating
mashed potatoes and vegetables.
Mrs Clements is fetching the chicken to
eat with it.

Albania

Entela Kopliku lives with her husband, Rifat, and his parents. She has a daughter, Doris. Entela walks to school. It takes about 20 minutes to get there.

The school day lasts from 8.30 am to 3 pm. The children have lunch at 12.30 pm.

Here the whole **class** is working quietly. The children sit in **rows**. They work at their desks all the time. They do not move to a carpet for a story or a lesson.

Entela sits at her desk. She goes around the class to see how the **students** are getting on. She teaches them to read, write and do maths. She also teaches them some geography and history.

The children play outside at playtime, if the weather is good. There is always a teacher in the playground to look after them.

Here two boys have been fighting. Entela has stopped them. She asks them why they were fighting, and if she can help.

Entela and Rifat eat their main meal at
work in the middle of the day. Rifat's
parents and Doris eat at home in the
middle of the day too. Sunday is the
one day they eat a main meal together.

Here they are eating meat, potatoes
and vegetables. After this they will eat
some fruit.

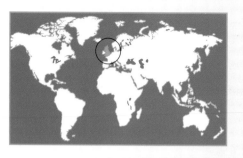

United Kingdom

Ian Blakesley lives about an hour's drive away from his school. The school day lasts from 8.45 am to 3.15 pm. The children have their lunch in the middle of the day, from 12 o'clock until 12.55 pm.

Here Ian is teaching the whole **class**. He does not always do this. Sometimes he teaches smaller groups.

Ian teaches his **students** to read, write and do maths. Some of the other things he teaches them are history, science, **P.E.** and geography.

Sometimes Ian sits at his desk while the whole **class** works. **Students** who have a question, or who have finished their work, come to the desk. Ian looks at their work with them.

Here Ian is checking Vicky's work. He talks to her about what she has done and what to do next.

Ian's wife, Anthea, teaches children to play musical instruments. She works at different schools each day. Anthea's parents look after the baby, Ceiridwen, while Anthea works.

The family eat their main meal together in the evening. Here they are eating fish, chips and peas.

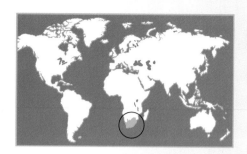

South Africa

Sylvia Daniels lives just 10 minutes' walk from her school. Her sons, Marlon and Ricardo, have grown up and left school.

The school day lasts from 8 am to 2.15 pm. The children have lunch in the middle of the day, at 12.30 pm.

Sylvia teaches her students to read, write and do maths. She teaches in two languages – English and **Afrikaans**.

Sylvia teaches her class everything else, too. They learn music, history, science, geography, and **P.E.** Here she is teaching maths to a group of students. Sometimes she teaches the whole class.

Here Sylvia is helping two of her **students** with an art **project**. She will go around the classroom and see how everyone is doing on their project.

While everyone is working happily on their projects, Sylvia can sit down and hear some children read to her.

The family eat their main meal in the evening. They are eating minced meat and mashed potatoes, rice, pumpkins and **mealies**. After this they will eat **sago pudding**.

Factfile

Albania

Population: 3½ million

Capital city: Tirana

United Kingdom (UK)

Population: 58 million

Capital city: London

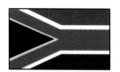

South Africa

Population: 44 million

Capital city: Pretoria

United States of America (USA)

Population: 264 million

Capital city: Washington DC

Digging Deeper

1   Look at page 3. What different ways of travelling can you see?

2   Look at page 5. What do you think the weather is like in Doncaster and in South Africa? Why?

3   Look at pages 7 and 11. How are the classrooms in the USA and Albania the same? How are they different?

Glossary

adventure playground an outdoor play area with things to climb and play on

Afrikaans a language that is widely spoken in South Africa. It is rather like Dutch, because many of the first white settlers in South Africa were Dutch.

class a group of children who all learn together with the same teacher

first grade a class for 6 and 7 year olds in the USA

local coming from the same area. In a village everyone in the village would be called a local person. Big towns or cities often have lots of smaller areas, each with 'local' names and local shops and schools.

mealies sweetcorn

mobile classroom a single classroom that is not a fixed building

P.E. physical education – activities like sports, dancing and swimming

primary school the first school that children go to in the UK and some other countries

rows things lined up in straight lines, one behind the other

sago pudding a pudding made with milk, sugar and small hard grains of the sago tree

student someone who goes somewhere (like a school or a college) to learn something

workbooks books with work for students to do and space for the work to be done. Each child can have their own workbook.

Index

First published in Great Britain by Heinemann Library
Halley Court, Jordan Hill, Oxford OX2 8EJ
a division of Reed Educational and Professional Publishing Ltd

OXFORD FLORENCE PRAGUE MADRID ATHENS MELBOURNE
AUCKLAND KUALA LUMPUR SINGAPORE TOKYO IBADAN
NAIROBI KAMPALA JOHANNESBURG GABORONE PORTSMOUTH
NH CHICAGO MEXICO CITY SAO PAULO

© Reed Educational and Professional Publishing Ltd 1996

Designed by John Walker

Illustrations by Oxford Illustrators and Visual Image

Printed in Malaysia

00 99 98 97 96
10 9 8 7 6 5 4 3 2 1

ISBN 0 431 06334 6

British Library Cataloguing in Publication Data

Hudson, Margaret

Teacher

I. Teachers – Juvenile literature

I. Title

630.9'2

Acknowledgements

The Publishers would like to thank the following for permission to reproduce photographs:

Roger Scruton: p 3 lower middle

Chris Honeywell: pp. 1, 5, 14–17;

Rhodri Jones/Oxfam: pp. 3, 4, 10–13;

Paul Grendon/Oxfam: pp. 3, 5, 18–21;

Steve Benbow: pp. 3, 4, 6–9

Cover photograph reproduced with permission of Steve Benbow.

Our thanks to Clare Boast for her comments in the preparation of this book.

Every effort has been made to contact copyright holders of any material reproduced in this book. Any omissions will be rectified in subsequent printings if notice is given to the Publisher.

Oxfam believes that all people have basic rights: to earn a living, to have food, shelter, health care and education. There are nine Oxfam organizations around the world - they work with poor people in over 70 countries. Oxfam provides relief in emergencies, and gives long term support to people who are working to make life better for themselves and their families.

Oxfam (UK and Ireland) produces a catalogue of resources for schools and young people. For a copy contact Oxfam, 274 Banbury Road, Oxford, OX2 7DZ (tel. 01865 311311) or contact your national Oxfam office.

Oxfam UK and Ireland is a Registered Charity number 202918. Oxfam UK and Ireland is a member of Oxfam International.